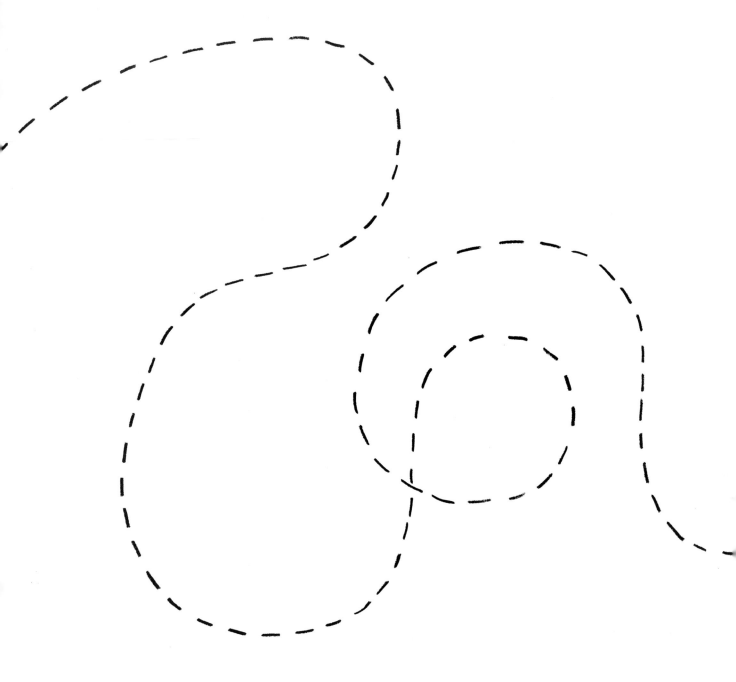

Ladybird books are widely available, but in case of difficulty may be ordered by post or telephone from:

Ladybird Books – Cash Sales Department Littlegate Road Paignton Devon TQ3 3BE
Telephone 01803 554761

A catalogue record for this book is available from the British Library

Published by Ladybird Books Ltd Loughborough Leicestershire UK
Ladybird Books Inc Auburn Maine 04210 USA

Copyright illustrations © Trevor Dunton MCMXCV
© LADYBIRD BOOKS LTD MCMXCV
LADYBIRD and the device of a Ladybird are trademarks of Ladybird Books Ltd
All rights reserved. No part of this publication may be reproduced, stored in a retrieval system, or transmitted in any form or by any means, electronic, mechanical, photocopying, recording or otherwise, without the prior consent of the copyright owners.

Shoo fly Shoo!

by Brian Moses
illustrated by Trevor Dunton

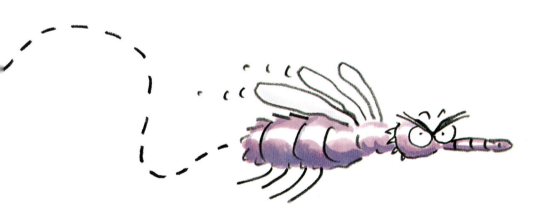

or give it a slap.

when it's taking a nap.

zzz z z z z Z Z Z

You can shout GET OUT...

and hope that it goes.

You can whack it with a bat...

when it lands on Dad's nose!

zzzz

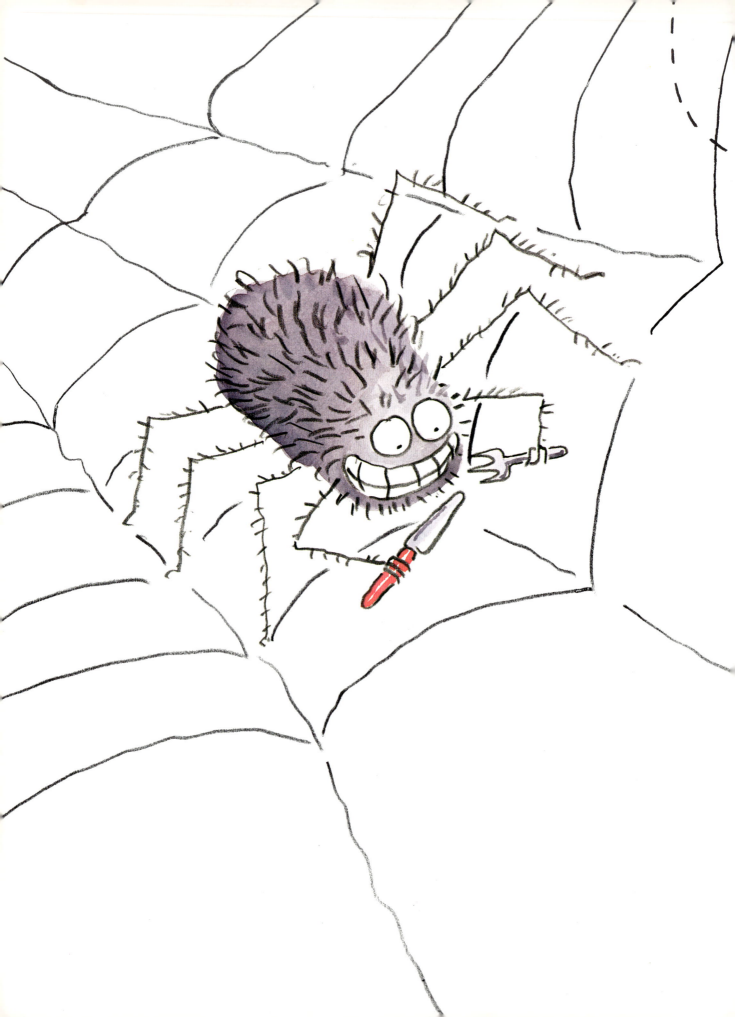

You can introduce it to a hungry spider...

or launch an attack with a paper glider.

and wave goodbye.

HERE IT IS

WAY OUT

BYE BYE FLY

THE DOOR

Or hope it meets up...

 with another fly.

But if all else fails and the fly flies away…

sit down, relax...

and have a nice...

GOT

CHA!